NATURE BOUND

WITH ____

WENAHA HENRY

UNFORGETTABLE ACTIVITIES TO IGNITE YOUR CHILD'S LOVE FOR THE GREAT OUTDOORS!

By

Emanuel Rose

Dedication

This book is dedicated to Richard Rose, my father and first mentor.

He taught me to build a fire, fly fish and enjoy the wild.

I think of him every time I go on a trip, no matter how short and miss his big presence and wry smile.

A portion of the proceeds from this book go to support Camp Jack Hazard, a nature and wilderness experience for kids.

Vocatus atque non vocatus deus aderit

Table of Contents

Forward

As a trained teacher, wilderness, and camping executive, I am delighted to introduce this book to you, which is an essential guide to experiencing the natural world and fostering a connection to nature. Written by Emanuel Rose, an experienced outdoor enthusiast. This book provides an engaging collection of activities and practical advice that will help you and your family create unforgettable memories in the great outdoors.

In today's fast-paced world, where technology dominates our lives, it is more important than ever to unplug and teach our children how to spend time in nature. Emanuel understands this, and through his own experiences, he has learned the many benefits of being in wild places. In this book, he shares his passion for nature and provides guidance on how to experience it in a fun, safe, and educational way.

From camping to mindfulness training, this book covers everything you need to know to plan your next outdoor adventure. With 50 activities to choose from, there is something for everyone, regardless of age or skill level. Whether you are a seasoned outdoor enthusiast or new to the world of camping and hiking, this book is an excellent resource for exploring the wonders of the natural world.

As a camp director, I believe that connecting with nature is essential for our mental and physical well-being. This book is an excellent resource for anyone looking to explore the great outdoors and connect with nature in a meaningful way. I highly recommend it to parents, educators, and anyone who wants to create lasting memories with their loved ones in the beauty of the natural world.

In conclusion, I applaud Emanuel for his dedication to sharing his passion for nature and for providing this valuable resource. I hope this book inspires you to venture outside, explore the wilderness, and connect with the natural world. Happy adventuring!

Jason Poisson
Executive Director Camp Jack Hazard
www.campjackhazard.org

Nature is the Social Media Addiction and Smartphone Antidote

As Tom Brown once said, "Nature is the ultimate teacher". Spending time in nature offers a respite from the constant stimulation of social media and phone addiction that plagues kids and teens.

In nature, kids and teens can engage in physical activity, breathe fresh air, connect with the natural world, problem solve straight forward situations and be in the "real world". This offers a much-needed break from the screen time that can negatively impact their brain chemistry, mental and physical health.

Nature provides a sense of calm and tranquility that can't be found in the constant chatter of social media. Being surrounded by trees, running water, and wildlife offers a sense of grounding and perspective that neutralizes the anxiety and stress of modern life.

Exploring the outdoors also fosters a sense of independence and self-sufficiency in kids and teens.

7

They learn to navigate their surroundings, make decisions, and rely on their own abilities, rather than constantly seeking the validation of social media likes and comments.

Overall, time spent in nature is a powerful antidote to the addictive and often overwhelming nature of social media and phone use. It offers a chance to disconnect, recharge, and cultivate a deeper sense of connection with the world around us.

Invite your children to experience the "real world" and build their sense of adventure!

Introduction

I am Emanuel Rose, the author of *Wenaha Henry*, a children's book series, wherein I have dedicated myself to sharing my passion and knowledge of the natural world with you. I believe that connecting with nature is a vital part of the human experience and that fostering this connection in our children and grandchildren is essential for their overall growth and well-being.

My first camping trip was when I was still a toddler, and my mother tied me to a tree next to a small creek while she was reading a book. While that style of parenting may be questionable, I am appreciative of the ethic of taking young children out into nature.

My first memory is of me catching a trout on a fly rod. No doubt my father had hooked it first and handed me the rod. There is a photo of me holding it at about 3 or 4 years old with the biggest smile on my face.

In my late teens and 20s, I worked at a summer camp in the High Sierra called Camp Jack Hazard. Every week we got to take kids from the central valley of California backpacking for at least three days and two nights. It was on those trips, seeing kids open up out in the wilderness, carrying their own gear and taking care of themselves, that I realized how universal the wilderness experience could be.

My dad passed away when I was in my mid-20s, but his love of camping and all outdoor pursuits and his desire to share them with me left an indelible mark. I remember many nights around a campfire, with my knife on my belt, recounting the day of hiking and fishing. Dad told me stories of his childhood and youth, building a connection that did not seem possible in our normal day-to-day life.

I have traveled all over the world to hike, fish, hunt, and backpack. I enjoy sunrises, solitude, and the pulse of nature because of the innumerable trips I went on alone, with friends and with my family. My commitment to myself is taking a minimum of one long weekend per month, sleeping in a sleeping bag and enjoying an adventure. In the spring, it is turkey hunting and fly fishing for trout; in summer, rafting and fishing; in fall, upland bird hunting; and in winter, waterfowl hunting and steelhead fishing.

Because of this commitment to the adventure, I pay attention to the weather, the rainfall totals, the animals, the forest fire situation, my hunting dog, and the season. I stay attuned as much as I can to the seasons and cycles to be prepared to be safe and have fun. My closest relationships are with the other people I enjoy these trips with, and they are as important to me as the trip itself is.

It is with great pleasure and a strong prayer for the future of humanity that I present to you this collection of inspiring, fun, and educational activities designed to help you and your children explore the wonders of the great outdoors together.

Nature, camping, hunting, and fishing have had a profound impact on my life. They have taught me valuable life lessons that have made me a better person. These experiences have taught me to be an active problem solver, be in good physical shape, appreciate nature, be comfortable alone, and respect the wilderness.

In nature, things don't always go according to plan. When things go wrong, I've learned to stay calm and think critically. Whether it's setting up camp in the rain or troubleshooting a broken fishing reel, I've learned to find creative solutions to problems.

These activities have also taught me the importance of being in good physical shape. Hiking through rugged terrain, carrying heavy gear, and casting a fishing rod for hours on end requires a certain level of physical fitness. Being in good shape has allowed me to enjoy these activities to the fullest and has given me the confidence to tackle new challenges.

Appreciating nature is another valuable lesson I've learned through camping, hunting, and fishing. Spending time in the great outdoors has given me a deep appreciation for the natural world. I've learned to observe and appreciate the beauty and complexity of the world around me.

Being comfortable alone is another lesson I've learned through these activities. Spending time in nature often means being alone with your thoughts. I've learned to appreciate solitude and use it as an opportunity for introspection and self-reflection.

Finally, these activities have taught me to respect the wilderness. Nature is a powerful force, and I've learned never to underestimate its power. I've also learned to minimize my impact on the environment and leave no trace behind.

Nature, camping, hunting, and fishing have had a profound impact on my life. I have fond memories of my family on camping and fishing trips, learned to survive in cold, rain and heat, and developed a deep appreciation for solitude and wilderness.

In today's fast-paced, technology-driven world, it's easy for children to become disconnected from the natural environment. As parents and mentors, it's our responsibility to cultivate an appreciation for nature in our children and teach them the importance of preserving our planet for future generations. This list of activities has been carefully curated to provide you with a diverse range of experiences that will not only engage and entertain your kids but also help them develop a deep understanding and love for the natural world.

Through activities in nature, your children will be encouraged to use their senses, creativity, and curiosity as they explore the wilderness. They'll learn about local plants and animals, observe, and track wildlife, and gain valuable survival skills. They'll also have the opportunity to express themselves artistically by creating nature-inspired artwork, collages, and stories. By participating in these activities, your children will develop critical thinking, problem-solving, and observational skills that will serve them well in all aspects of life

Through my studies, I have gained an understanding of the importance of balancing structured activities with unstructured, free play. This list incorporates both types of experiences to provide a well-rounded and enriching outdoor experience for your kids. I encourage you to use these activities as a starting point and feel free to adapt them to suit the specific needs, interests, and abilities of your children. Remember that the goal is not to complete every activity on the list but rather to ignite a passion for the outdoors that will last a lifetime.

As you embark on these adventures with your children, I urge you to lead by example. Demonstrate your our own curiosity, excitement, and respect for nature, and your children will follow suit. Take the time to truly immerse yourselves in the experience, leaving behind the distractions of modern life, and you'll find that these shared moments in nature will create lifelong memories and strengthen the bond between you and your children.

This book was created to give you the tools and a few activities for you and your children to enjoy and to start leaving the electronic devices locked away and to fill some days with positive and rewarding shared experiences being Nature Bound.

In closing, I hope this list serves as a valuable resource and source of inspiration for you and your family. Remember that as parents, we have the incredible opportunity to instill a love for the natural world in our children that will shape their lives and the future of our planet. So, gather your little explorers, venture into the great outdoors, and let the magic of Mother Nature guide your journey.

Wishing you and your family endless adventures.

Emanuel Rose

Nature Bound Quick Start Guide

Introducing children to nature and activities such as rafting, backpacking, small-game and upland bird hunting, and fishing can be a rewarding and enriching experience. However, ensuring their comfort, safety, and enjoyment is crucial to fostering a love for these adventures. This quick start guide will provide essential tips for creating a memorable and enjoyable outdoor experience for children aged 5 to 10 years old.

1. Comfort is King: The Right Gear for a Positive Experience

To make sure that children have the best possible experience in the great outdoors, it is essential to prioritize their comfort. Start by selecting the appropriate clothing, footwear, and sleeping gear that will keep them warm, dry, and comfortable throughout the trip.

Clothing: Dress children in layers, as this allows them to adjust easily to changing temperatures. Choose moisture-wicking materials that dry quickly. Avoid cotton, which can retain moisture and cause chills. Waterproof jackets and pants are essential for rainy conditions, while sun hats and sunscreen protect against sunburns.

Footwear: Invest in high-quality hiking boots or shoes that provide good support and traction. Make sure they are the correct size and are properly broken in before the trip to prevent blisters and discomfort.

Sleeping gear: Choose a child-friendly sleeping bag with the appropriate temperature rating for the conditions. A comfortable sleeping pad and pillow can make a significant difference in sleep quality, ensuring children wake up refreshed and ready for another day of adventure.

2. Pack the Snacks: Fueling Young Explorers

Children require plenty of energy to enjoy their outdoor activities, so packing tasty and nutritious snacks is a must. Focus on high-energy items that travel well and can be easily consumed on the go, even in warm weather.

Juice boxes and water bottles: Hydration is crucial for maintaining energy levels and preventing fatigue. Pack a variety of drinks to keep kids interested and encourage them to drink regularly.

Granola bars, trail mix, and dried fruit: These snacks are easy to pack and provide a quick energy boost when needed. They are also less likely to spoil in warm temperatures.

Crackers, cheese, and fruit: A mix of salty and sweet snacks can help keep children satisfied and engaged throughout the day.

3. **Kids Rule: Embrace Their Interests and Encourage Exploration**

When participating in outdoor activities with children, it is important to remember that the focus should be on their interests and enjoyment. Encourage them to explore the aspects of the outdoors that interest them, and be prepared to adjust your plans to suit their preferences.

Give children the freedom to choose which activities they would like to try and be open to new experiences.

Allow for unstructured playtimes, such as throwing rocks, skipping stones, or simply splashing in a stream. This can provide valuable opportunities for creativity, curiosity, and self-discovery.

Be patient and understanding, and remember that the goal is to create positive memories that will encourage a lifelong love of outdoor adventure.

4. Have Fun or Be Done: Respect Their Boundaries and Know When to Call It a Day

While it is essential to encourage children to try new things and push their limits, it is equally important to recognize their boundaries and respect their wishes. If a child expresses a desire to return to the car or go home, it is best to honor that request.

Listen to their concerns and offer support, but do not force them to continue if they are genuinely uncomfortable or unhappy.

Be prepared to cut the trip short if necessary and focus on the positive aspects of the experience. Discuss what they enjoyed and what they might like to try next time.

Remember that the primary goal is to foster a love for outdoor adventure. Forcing children to stay longer than they want to can have the opposite effect, making them less likely to want to participate in the future.

Creating positive and memorable outdoor experiences for children aged 5 to 10 is crucial for nurturing their love for adventure and fostering skill development and psychological growth. By prioritizing comfort, packing the right snacks, embracing their interests, and respecting their boundaries, you can ensure that your young

Keep the following Nature Bound Checklist's four essential tips in mind as you plan your next adventure, and watch as your children flourish in the wonder and excitement of nature.

Nature Bound Checklist

1. Comfort is King
- Layered clothing with moisture-wicking materials
- Waterproof jackets and pants
- Sun protection (hats, sunscreen)
- High-quality, properly fitted hiking boots
- Child-friendly sleeping gear (bag, pad, pillow)

2. Pack the Snacks
- Juice boxes and water bottles for hydration
- Granola bars, trail mix, and dried fruit for energy
- Crackers, cheese, and fruit for variety

3. Kids Rule
- Let children choose activities
- Encourage unstructured playtime
- Be patient and understanding
- Focus on positive memories

4. Have Fun or Be Done
- Listen to and respect children's boundaries

- Offer support but don't force participation
- Be prepared to cut the trip short if needed
- Focus on fostering a love for outdoor adventure

Notes and Plans

Essential Gear for Nature Excursions with Your 5- to 10-Year-Old Kids

Introducing your 5- to 10-year-old kids to the wonders of nature can be an incredibly rewarding experience for the entire family. To ensure that your outdoor adventures are safe, comfortable, and enjoyable, it's essential to pack the right gear. In this section, we'll cover the must-have items you'll need to take your little explorers on unforgettable nature excursions.

1. Backpacks: A comfortable, well-fitting backpack is essential for carrying supplies during your nature outings. Choose age-appropriate, lightweight backpacks for your kids, and ensure they fit correctly and are adjusted to distribute the weight evenly. Kids can carry their snacks, water bottles, and small personal items, while adults can carry the bulk of the gear.

2. Clothing: Dressing in layers is crucial for adapting to changing weather conditions and maintaining comfort throughout the day. Opt for moisture-wicking, quick-drying fabrics, and avoid cotton as it retains moisture and can lead to discomfort or hypothermia. Key clothing items include:

- **Base layer:** moisture-wicking shirts and leggings
- **Insulating layer:** fleece jackets or vests
- **Outer layer:** waterproof and breathable jackets and pants
- **Hats:** sun hats for warm weather and warm beanies for colder conditions
- **Gloves:** lightweight gloves for sun protection or insulated gloves for cold weather
- **Socks:** moisture-wicking, quick-drying socks (bring extras in case they get wet)
- **Footwear:** sturdy, closed-toe shoes or hiking boots with good traction

3. First Aid Kit: Accidents can happen, so always carry a well-stocked first aid kit. Include adhesive bandages, gauze pads, antiseptic wipes, tweezers, pain relievers, any necessary prescription medications, and a compact first aid guide.

4. Navigation Tools: Familiarize yourself with the area you'll be exploring and carry a map, compass, or GPS device. Teach your children basic map-reading and navigation skills to foster their sense of responsibility and self-reliance.

5. Hydration: Staying hydrated is critical, especially for young children who may not always recognize when they're thirsty. Bring enough water for the duration of your outing and consider using hydration packs or water bottles with built-in filters for easy access and refilling in natural water sources.

6. Snacks and Meals: Pack nutritious, high-energy snacks like trail mix, granola bars, and fruit to keep energy levels up during your excursion. For longer outings or overnight trips, bring easy-to-prepare, lightweight meals like dehydrated meals, instant soups, or pasta.

7. Sun Protection: Apply sunscreen with at least SPF 30 to exposed skin and reapply as needed. Equip your kids with sunglasses and wide-brimmed hats to protect their eyes and faces from the sun.

8. Insect Repellent: Use insect repellent to protect against mosquito and tick bites. Choose child-friendly options with natural ingredients or low concentrations of DEET.

9. Emergency Whistle: Give each child an emergency whistle to use in case they become separated from the group. Teach them to blow the whistle in a series of three short blasts to signal for help.

10. Multi-tool or Pocket Knife: Carry a multi-tool or pocket knife for various tasks, such as cutting rope or opening packages. Ensure the tool is kept in a safe place and that children are taught proper handling and usage.

11. Flashlihts and Headlamps: Equip each family member with a flashlight or headlamp in case you're out after dark. Choose models with long battery life, and pack extra batteries.

12. Weather Protection: Bring compact, lightweight rain ponchos or umbrellas for unexpected rain showers. For colder weather excursions, pack hand warmers and extra insulating layers to keep everyone warm and comfortable.

13. Outdoor Seating: Bring portable, lightweight seating options such as foldable chairs, foam pads, or compact inflatable cushions. These will provide a comfortable place to rest during breaks and help keep everyone dry and clean when sitting on the ground.

14. Binoculars and Field Guides: Equip your kids with binoculars and age-appropriate field guides to encourage exploration and learning about local flora and fauna. This will help them develop an appreciation for their surroundings and foster a sense of curiosity and wonder.

15. Camera or Smartphone: Capture the memories of your nature excursions by bringing a camera or smartphone to take photos. Encourage your children to document their discoveries and experiences, creating a visual record of their adventures.

16. Entertainment and Educational Items: Pack lightweight, nature-themed books, playing cards, or small games to keep kids entertained during downtime or rest periods. Consider bringing a sketchbook and colored pencils for children to draw their observations and surroundings.

17. *Leave No Trace* **Gear:** Teach your kids the importance of practicing *Leave No Trace* principles by bringing along a small trash bag for collecting litter and a trowel for digging catholes when nature calls. Encourage them to respect and care for the environment they're exploring.

By packing the right gear and planning your nature excursions carefully, you'll be well-prepared to create memorable outdoor experiences with your 5- to 10-year-old kids. These outings will not only strengthen your family bond but also instill a lifelong appreciation for nature and the great outdoors in your children.

A Guide to Camping with Your 5- to 10-Year-Old Kids: Preparing for a Memorable Adventure

Taking your children camping is an excellent way to bond as a family, create lifelong memories, and instill a love for nature. To ensure a successful and enjoyable experience, it's essential to plan and prepare carefully. In this guide, we'll discuss what you should do before, during, and after a camping trip with your 5- to 10-year-old kids.

Before the Camping Trip:

1. **Choose the right campground:** Research campgrounds that cater to families with young children. Look for facilities with amenities such as playgrounds, easy access to restrooms, and gentle hiking trails. Read reviews from other families to ensure the campground is suitable for your children's age group. If you want to avoid other people and campgrounds, look for BLM land on Google Maps or OnX.

2. **Make reservations:** Popular campgrounds can fill up quickly, so book your campsite well in advance.

Choose a site that offers some shade, is close to rest-rooms and water sources, and provides a flat area for setting up tents.

3. Plan your meals: Create a meal plan for the duration of your trip, taking into account any dietary restrictions or preferences. Opt for simple, easy-to-prepare meals that require minimal cooking and cleanup. Pre-measure and pack ingredients in reusable containers or ziplock bags to save time and reduce waste.

4. Pack the essentials: Ensure you have all the necessary gear and supplies, including a tent, sleeping bags, sleeping pads, cooking equipment, clothing, a first aid kit, and any required permits. Use a comprehensive packing list to avoid forgetting essential items.

5. Prepare for emergencies: Familiarize yourself with the location of the nearest hospital, park ranger station, and emergency phone numbers. Make sure your first aid kit is well-stocked, and teach your children basic safety precautions and what to do in case of an emergency.

6. Practice setting up your gear: Before embarking on your trip, set up your tent and practice using your camping equipment with your children. This will help familiarize them with the process and ensure a smoother experience once you're at the campsite.

During the Camping Trip:

1. Set up camp: Upon arrival, set up your tent and organize your campstie. Assign tasks to your children, such as unrolling sleeping bags or setting up chairs, to help them feel involved and responsible.

2. Establish a routine: Create a daily schedule that includes meal times, planned activities, and quiet time. Having a routine will help maintain a sense of structure and familiarity for your children.

3. Stay safe: Teach your children the importance of following safety rules at the campsite. These may include keeping a safe distance from the campfire, not wandering off alone, and properly storing food to avoid attracting wildlife.

4. Plan fun and educational activities: Engage your kids in nature-related activities such as hiking, bird-watching, scavenger hunts, or fishing. Bring along field guides and binoculars to encourage learning and exploration.

5. Encourage campfire bonding: Spend evenings around the campfire, sharing stories, singing songs, and roasting marshmallows for s'mores. This will create a cozy atmosphere and strengthen family bonds.

6. Practice *Leave No Trace* principles: Teach your children to respect the environment by packing out trash, minimizing their impact on nature, and leaving the campsite cleaner than they found it.

After the Camping Trip:

1. Clean and store your gear: Upon returning home, clean and dry all your camping equipment before storing it away. This will help prolong the lifespan of your gear and ensure it's ready for your next adventure.

2. Reflect on your experience: Discuss your camping trip as a family, reflecting on your favorite moments, what you learned, and what you'd like to do differently.

Notes and Plans

Planning Your Family's Adventure

When planning a wilderness adventure with your 5- to 10-year-old children, it is crucial to find an area that is safe, age-appropriate, and engaging for the whole family. Include your kids in the planning process, shopping and packing so they get experience with all of those activities. Also, give them tasks to complete with and without your help to make the pre-trip successful!

Here are the steps a mother can take to find the perfect wilderness areas for her kids:

1. **Research local parks, BLM, National Forests, National Parks, and nature reserves:** Start by looking for parks, nature reserves, and wilderness areas in your local vicinity. Many towns and cities have designated green spaces and conservation areas that can provide a great introduction to nature for young children. Search online, visit your local library, or contact your local government office for information about nearby parks and nature reserves.

2. Consult friends and family: Ask friends, family members, and acquaintances with kids for recommendations on their favorite wilderness spots. They may have insights on locations that are particularly kid-friendly and engaging.

3. Utilize online resources and forums: There are numerous smartphone apps that can help you find and navigate wilderness areas. Some popular options include OnX, AllTrails, Gaia GPS, and REI's Hiking Project. These apps provide trail maps, user reviews, photos, and other valuable information to help you find the perfect spot for your family outing.

4. Consult guidebooks and maps: Local bookstores, outdoor stores, and libraries often carry guidebooks and maps for nearby wilderness areas. These resources can offer valuable insights into the terrain, difficulty, and features of various trails and parks. Topographical maps can be particularly useful for understanding the elevation changes and terrain of a specific area.

5. Connect with local outdoor communities: Reach out to local hiking clubs, outdoor organizations, and hunting associations through their social media groups. It is a great way to gain firsthand knowledge and recommendations from experienced outdoor enthusiasts in your area. They can often provide insider tips and advice on the best wilderness areas for families with young children.

6. **Visit outdoor stores:** Outdoor stores like REI, Bass Pro Shops, and Cabela's typically have knowledgeable staff who can help you find wilderness areas based on your specific needs and preferences. They may also host workshops or events related to outdoor activities for families and children.

7. **Contact park rangers and visitor centers:** Once you've identified a few potential wilderness areas, reach out to park rangers or visitor centers to gather additional information. They can provide insight into the suitability of the area for young children, any potential hazards, and the best times to visit.

8. **Check weather conditions and park alerts:** Before finalizing your plans, check the weather forecast and park alerts for your chosen wilderness area. This will help you avoid any unexpected closures or

hazardous conditions that may impact your outing.

9. Plan your visit: Once you've identified the perfect wilderness area, create a detailed plan for your visit. Include information such as travel time, parking, entrance fees, and any necessary permits. Be sure to pack appropriate gear, clothing, and supplies for your chosen activities.

10. Be prepared for the unexpected: When venturing into the wilderness with young children, it's essential to be prepared for the unexpected. Bring a well-stocked first aid kit, extra food and water, and a map and compass or GPS device for navigation. Ensure that you and your children are familiar with basic safety precautions and what to do in case of an emergency.

By following these steps, you'll be well-equipped to find the perfect wilderness area for your family to explore and create lasting memories together in the great outdoors.

50 Outdoor Activities for Your 5- to 10-Year-Old Child

1. Nature scavenger hunt: Prepare a list of common items found in nature (leaves, rocks, pinecones, etc.) and have your children search for them.

2. Birdwatching: Teach kids to identify local bird using a bird guide and binoculars.

3. Leaf rubbing: Have kids collect different leaves and use crayons to create leaf rubbings on paper.

4. Rock painting: Collect rocks and have your children paint them with non-toxic, washable paints.

5. Animal tracking: Teach children how to identify and follow animal tracks in the wilderness.

6. Bug exploration: Observe and learn about insects found in the area using a magnifying glass for close-up inspection.

7. Nature journaling: Encourage children to draw and

write about their experiences and observations in nature.

8. Sensory walk: Have kids walk through the forest while focusing on different senses, such as touch, smell, and sound.

9. Plant identification: Teach kids to identify local plants using a field guide.

10. Nature photography: Provide your children with cameras and encourage them to take pictures of the natural world.

11. Wildlife observation: Teach your children how to safely observe and learn about the animals they encounter in nature.

12. Build a shelter: Use fallen branches and leaves to create a small fort or shelter in the woods. If you want to be real cool, spend the night in it with them.

13. Cloud watching: Lie on the grass and have your children use their imagination to find shapes and stories in the clouds.

14. Create nature mandalas: Arrange natural materials, such as stones, leaves, and flowers, into mandalas or other patterns.

15. Make a sunprint: Use sun-sensitive paper and natural materials to create unique artwork.

16. Nature-inspired storytelling: Encourage your children to create stories based on their experiences and observations in nature.

17. Pond dipping: Use nets to catch and release aquatic creatures for observation and identification.

18. Build a mini ecosystem: Create a small terrarium using local plants and soil, teaching children about ecosystems and their inhabitants.

19. Wind observations: Use pinwheels or ribbons to observe and discuss the wind and its effects on the environment.

20. Tree rubbing: Use crayons or charcoal to make rubbings of tree bark and compare the different textures.

21. Make nature collages: Collect natural materials and have your children create collages on paper or cardboard.

22. Build a bug hotel: Construct a simple bug hotel using sticks, bark, and other natural materials to attract and observe insects.

23. Nature-themed obstacle course: Set up a fun and challenging obstacle course using natural elements like logs, rocks, and hills.

24. Rainy day exploration: Embrace wet weather by exploring nature during a gentle rain, teaching your children about the water cycle and the importance of rain for the ecosystem.

25. Nature-based mindfulness: Practice mindfulness and meditation techniques while immersed in nature, helping your children develop a deeper connection to the environment.

26. Animal track casting: Teach your children how to create plaster casts of animal tracks they find in the wild. This helps them learn about the animals that live in the area and creates a lasting memento of their outdoor adventure.

27. Track comparison game: Gather various animal track images or drawings and have kids match them to their respective animals. This will familiarize them with common local wildlife and their tracks.

28. Animal track storytelling: Encourage your children to observe a series of animal tracks and use their imaginations to create a story about what the animal was doing. This helps them learn about animal behavior and improves their creative story-telling skills.

29. Track-based scavenger hunt: Create a scavenger hunt based on specific animal tracks that the children must find and identify. This activity encourages observation skills and introduces kids to various animal species in the area.

30. Mud tracking station: Set up a shallow container filled with mud or damp sand, then have kids create animal tracks using toy animals, track stamps, or their hands. This helps them understand how tracks are formed and practice identifying different tracks in a controlled environment.

31. Nature yoga: Teach your children simple yoga poses inspired by animals and plants, helping them to connect with nature while improving their flexibility and balance.

32. Weather observations: Guide children in observing and recording the weather, teaching them about different types of clouds, temperature changes, and weather patterns.

33. Star gazing: Introduce kids to the wonders of the night sky by identifying constellations and learning about the myths and stories behind them.

34. Nature-based science experiments: Conduct simple science experiments using natural materials, such as testing the pH of the soil or exploring the properties of different rocks.

35. Hiking: Choose age-appropriate trails and embark on guided hikes, teaching your children about trail etiquette and the importance of staying on marked paths. Make sure they carry their own in water and snacks at least.

36. Geocaching: Combine technology and nature by participating in a geocaching adventure, where children can search for hidden treasures using GPS coordinates.

37. Make natural dyes: Teach your children how to create natural dyes using plants, flowers, and berries, and use the dyes to color fabric or paper.

38. Nature relay races: Organize relay races that incorporate natural materials and tasks, such as balancing a pinecone on a spoon or collecting a specific number of leaves.

39. Nature-inspired crafts: Guide children in creating crafts using materials found in nature, such as twig picture frames, flower pressing, or leaf crowns.

40. Orienteering: Teach your children basic map reading and navigation skills, and practice orienteering in a safe, controlled environment.

41. Fishing: Introduce kids to the joys of fishing, teaching them about local fish species, fishing techniques, and the importance of catch and release.

42. Canoeing or kayaking: Explore local waterways by canoe or kayak, teaching your children about water safety and the importance of protecting aquatic ecosystems.

43. Making nature-inspired musical instruments: Create simple musical instruments using natural materials, such as seed shakers or stick drums, and encourage your children to make music together.

44. Environmental stewardship activities: Engage your children in activities that promote environmental stewardship, such as planting trees, picking up litter, or removing invasive species.

45. Create nature-based art installations: Guide your children in creating temporary, eco-friendly art installations using natural materials, such as stick sculptures or flower arrangements.

46. Make a nature mosaic: Collect a variety of natural materials and have your children create a mosaic on the ground, showcasing their creativity and appreciation for nature's beauty.

47. Nature-inspired charades: Play a game of charades using nature-themed prompts, encouraging your children to act out various animals, plants, or natural phenomena.

48. Forest bathing: Practice the Japanese art of shinrin-yoku, or forest bathing, by encouraging your children to mindfully experience nature through all their senses.

49. Nature memory game: Collect various natural objects and create a memory game by hiding the items under cups, then having children try to find and remember the matching pairs.

50. Nature-based sensory bins: Create sensory bins filled with natural materials, such as sand, water, leaves, or stones, allowing children to explore different textures and sensations while learning about nature.

Notes and Plans

Meditation Practices, Night Hikes and Periods of Isolation

Teaching children meditation in a forest setting can be a fun and engaging way to introduce them to mindfulness and relaxation. Here are three activities to help you get started:

1. Forest Breathing Exercise:

Start by finding a quiet spot in the forest where you both can sit comfortably. Ask your child to close their eyes and take deep, slow breaths. Guide them to inhale deeply through their nose, then exhale slowly through their mouth. Encourage them to pay attention to the sounds of the forest — the rustling leaves, birds singing, and the wind blowing. By focusing on their breath and the surrounding sounds, the child will begin to develop an awareness of the present moment and learn to calm their mind.

2. Nature Walk and Mindful Observation:

Take a leisurely walk through the forest with your child, encouraging them to observe their surroundings mindfully. Ask them to notice the different colors, textures, and shapes of leaves, flowers, and trees. Encourage them to touch the bark of a tree or feel the texture of a leaf. Periodically, stop and ask your child to close their eyes, take a few deep breaths, and then continue walking. This activity helps the child connect with nature while also developing their ability to focus and be present at the moment.

3. Forest Gratitude Circle:

Find a comfortable spot in the forest and sit together in a circle. Ask your children to think about three things they are grateful for in nature. It could be the warmth of the sun, the sound of a babbling brook, or the sight of a beautiful flower. Take turns sharing your gratitude, and after each person shares, take a deep breath together. This activity encourages the children to appreciate the beauty of nature and cultivate a sense of gratitude, which is an important aspect of mindfulness practice.

4. A Moonlight Walk:

A moonlight walk in the forest can be a magical and memorable experience for both parents and children. It offers an opportunity to explore nature, develop mindfulness, and foster a deeper connection with the environment. To ensure a safe and enjoyable moonlight walk for a 5- to 10-year-old child, follow these instructions:

Choose the right night: Pick a night with a bright moon (preferably a full moon) and clear skies to ensure maximum visibility. Check the local weather forecast to avoid any unexpected rain or storms.

Pick a safe location: Choose a well-known, familiar forest or park with established trails that you've visited during daylight hours. This will help minimize the risk of getting lost or encountering any hazards.

Plan your route: Plan a short and easy route, taking into account your child's age, stamina, and walking abilities. Make sure to familiarize yourself with the trail and any important land-marks before the walk.

Dress appropriately: Ensure that both you and your child are dressed in warm, comfortable clothing and sturdy footwear. Bring extra layers to account for temperature drops during the night. Use reflective gear or brightly colored clothing to increase visibility.

Pack essential supplies: Bring a small back pack with essential items such as a fully charged flashlight or headlamp (to use only in case of emergency or when absolutely necessary), a whistle, a first aid kit, water, and some light snacks.

Discuss safety rules: Before setting out on your walk, discuss safety rules with your child. Remind them to stay close to you at all times, follow the established trail, and avoid touching or picking up unfamiliar objects or plants.

Engage the senses: Encourage your child to

use their senses while walking. Ask them to listen to the sounds of the forest, feel the textures of leaves or bark, and observe the way the moonlight illuminates their surroundings.

Play games and tell stories: To keep your child engaged and entertained during the walk, consider playing games like "I Spy" or sharing stories related to the forest, moon, or stars.

Practice mindfulness: Periodically, pause and encourage your child to take deep breaths, focusing on the sensations of their breath and the sounds of the forest at night. This will help promote mindfulness and relaxation.

Reflect and share: After the walk, spend some time together reflecting on the experience. Ask your child about their favorite parts of the walk, what they learned, and how they felt during the experience.

If you follow these instructions, you can create a safe and enjoyable moonlight walk in the forest that can help foster a love for nature, develop mindfulness skills, and create lasting memories for both you and your child.

By incorporating these activities into your forest visit, you will provide a gentle introduction to meditation and mindfulness for your child. As they engage in the activities, they will learn to connect with nature, develop a sense of gratitude, and practice being present at the moment. Over time, these skills will lay the foundation for a lifelong practice of mindfulness and meditation that can support their emotional and mental well-being throughout their lives. Remember to be patient and keep the activities age-appropriate, making sure to maintain a playful and relaxed atmosphere to ensure a positive experience for your child.

5. Lone Sit Activity:

A "lone sit" activity allows your child to spend some quiet time alone in nature, fostering their sense of independence, observation skills, and mindfulness. To create a safe and enjoyable lone sit activity for a 5-year-old child, follow these steps:

Choose a suitable location: Find a safe and comfortable spot in the forest, preferably within your line of sight. Ensure the area is free of hazards, such as steep slopes, poisonous plants, or insects. If possible, pick a spot with some natural boundaries, like a small clearing or a space between trees, to create a sense of security.

Prepare the child: Explain the purpose of the lone sit activity to the child, emphasizing that it's a special time for them to enjoy nature by themselves. Set a specific duration for the activity, such as 5-10 minutes, which is appropriate for their age and attention span.

Create a comfortable space: Help your child set up a comfortable sitting area using a small cushion, blanket, or mat. This will encourage them to remain seated and focused during the activity.

Set ground rules: Before the child begins their lone sit, establish some ground rules to ensure their safety. Explain that they should stay within the designated area and avoid touching or eating anything they find in the forest. Make sure they understand they can call you if they feel uncomfortable or need assistance.

Offer guidance: Encourage your child to use their senses to observe the environment during their lone sit. Suggest that they listen to the sounds of the forest, feel the texture of the ground or leaves, and observe the colors and shapes of the plants and animals around them.

Remain nearby: While the child is engaged in their lone sit, stay within earshot to ensure their safety. Use this time for your own meditation or quiet reflection, but be prepared to respond if your child needs assistance.

Reflection and sharing: Once the lone sit is over, join your child and ask them about their experience. Encourage them to share what they observed, how they felt, and what they learned during their time alone in the forest.

Incorporate a lone sit activity into your forest visit. You may foster your child's independence, observation skills, and connection with nature.

Remember to emphasize safety and provide clear guidance to ensure a positive experience. As your child becomes more comfortable with the activity, you can gradually increase the duration of the lone sit, further developing their mindfulness and meditation skills. Ask your child questions like "What did you hear?" "How many different animals do they think you heard?" and "Did you see anything cool?"

NATURE BOUND with WENAHA HENRY
Emanuel Rose

Notes and Plans

660

Nurturing Young Minds and Bodies through Adventure

Nature has always been an essential part of human life, and there is no better way to connect with it than through outdoor activities such as white water rafting, backpacking, small game hunting, and fishing. Engaging children aged 5 to 10 in these activities not only provides them with valuable experiences and memories but also contributes to their skill development and psychological growth.

1. White Water Rafting: Building Teamwork and Courage

Rafting is an exhilarating water sport that teaches young children the importance of teamwork and communication. Navigating through rapids and around obstacles requires coordination and cooperation among raft members, which can help children develop essential social skills. Furthermore, rafting exposes children to the beauty of rivers and the surrounding environment, fostering a deep appreciation for nature.

Children who participate in rafting learn to confront their fears and overcome challenges, building confidence and resilience. As they navigate the rapids, they develop their problem-solving skills and learn the value of perseverance, traits that can serve them well in many aspects of life.

2. Backpacking: Fostering Independence and Responsibility

Backpacking offers children the opportunity to explore nature while learning valuable life skills. The physical demands of hiking and carrying a back-pack instill a sense of responsibility and discipline, as children must manage their energy, belongings, and well-being.

Backpacking also encourages children to become more self-reliant and independent. They learn to read maps, navigate trails, and make decisions based on their instincts and observations. Furthermore, they gain a sense of accomplishment when they reach their destination, boosting their self-esteem and confidence. Backpacking with other children or family members allows them to build social connections, fostering healthy relationships.

3. Hunting: Instilling Patience and Respect for Wildlife

Hunting introduces children to firearms, the world of wildlife and the importance of conservation. Through responsible hunting practices, children learn to handle a firearm safely, respect the balance of eco-systems and the role that animals play in maintaining them. They gain a deeper understanding of nature and our interconnectedness with the environment.

Hunting also teaches children patience and focus, as they must wait quietly for the right opportunity to present itself. These skills can translate to improved attention and concentration in other aspects of their lives. Additionally, hunting encourages physical fitness and coordination, as children must traverse various terrains and develop their marksmanship.

4. Fishing: Cultivating Mindfulness and Relaxation

Fishing is a timeless activity that offers children a chance to unwind and connect with the natural world. The tranquil surroundings of lakes and rivers provide a peaceful setting for children to practice mindfulness and relaxation, essential components of mental health and well-being.

Fishing teaches children the importance of patience, as they must wait for fish to bite. This practice can help them develop better impulse control and emotional regulation, which are crucial life skills. Moreover, the excitement of reeling in a fish can boost their self-confidence and sense of accomplishment.

Outdoor activities like rafting, backpacking, small game hunting, and fishing offer children aged 5 to 10 a world of adventure and learning opportunities. Participating in these activities nurtures their skill development and psychological growth, fostering essential traits like teamwork, independence, patience, and respect for nature. By engaging in these activities, children not only create lifelong memories but also build a strong foundation for a healthy, balanced, and fulfilling life.

Notes and Plans

Fireside Favorites:
Classic Campfire Meals and Snacks

Campfire Hot Dogs

- Hot dogs
- Hot dog buns
- Condiments (ketchup, mustard, relish)

Skewer hot dogs on roasting sticks and cook them over the campfire until they're cooked through and slightly charred. Serve on buns with desired condiments.

Campfire Foil Packets

- Protein (chicken, ground beef, or tofu)
- Vegetables (potatoes, carrots, bell peppers, onions)
- Olive oil
- Salt, pepper, and favorite seasonings

Place the protein and chopped vegetables on a large piece of aluminum foil. Drizzle with olive oil and season with salt, pepper, and your favorite seasonings. Fold the foil into a sealed packet and cook it over the campfire for 20-30 minutes, occasionally turning, until everything is cooked through.

Grilled Cheese Sandwiches

- Bread
- Cheese (cheddar, Swiss, or mozzarella)
- Butter

Butter one side of each slice of bread. Place cheese between the slices, with the buttered sides facing out. Wrap the sandwich in foil and cook it over the campfire for 3-4 minutes per side or until the cheese is melted and the bread is golden brown.

Campfire Nachos

- Tortilla chips
- Shredded cheese (cheddar or Monterey Jack)
- Toppings (black beans, diced tomatoes, jalapeños, olives)
- Aluminum pie plate or cast iron skillet

Layer tortilla chips, cheese, and desired toppings in an aluminum pie plate or cast iron skillet. Cover with foil and cook over the campfire for 5-10 minutes until the cheese is melted.

S'mores

- Graham crackers
- Chocolate bars
- Marshmallows

Roast marshmallows over the campfire until golden brown and gooey. Sandwich the roasted marshmallow and a piece of chocolate between two graham crackers.

Campfire Banana Boats

- Bananas
- Chocolate chips
- Mini marshmallows

Make a slit in a banana, leaving the peel on. Stuff the banana with chocolate chips and mini marshmallows. Wrap the banana in foil and cook it over the campfire for 5-10 minutes until the chocolate and marshmallows are melted.

Campfire Pizza

- Pizza dough or pre-made crust
- Pizza sauce
- Mozzarella cheese
- Toppings (pepperoni, mushrooms, olives)

Roll out the pizza dough and place it in a greased cast iron skillet. Top with pizza sauce, cheese, and desired toppings. Cook over the campfire for 15-20 minutes until the crust is golden and the cheese is melted.

Campfire Popcorn

- Popcorn kernels
- Oil or butter
- Salt

Place popcorn kernels and oil or butter in a heavy-duty foil pouch. Seal the pouch tightly, leaving room for the popcorn to expand. Shake the pouch over the campfire until it is fully popped. Season with salt.

Campfire Quesadillas

- Flour tortillas
- Shredded cheese (cheddar or Monterey Jack)
- Optional fillings (cooked chicken, black beans, diced tomatoes)

Place a tortilla on a piece of foil and add a layer of shredded cheese and desired fillings. Top with another tortilla and fold the foil to seal the quesadilla. Cook it over the campfire for 3-4 minutes per side until the cheese is melted and the tortillas are crispy.

Campfire Apple Crisp

- Apples, sliced
- Brown sugar
- Cinnamon
- Rolled oats
- Butter

Place sliced apples in a greased cast iron skillet or aluminum pie plate. In a separate bowl, mix together brown sugar, cinnamon, and rolled oats. Sprinkle this mixture over the apples. Dot the top with small pieces of butter. Cover the skillet or pie plate with foil and cook it over the campfire for 20-30 minutes, until the apples are tender and the topping is crispy. Enjoy your Campfire Apple Crisp warm, straight from the skillet or pie plate.

The Lasting Impact of Nature Adventures: Nurturing a Love for the Great Outdoors in Your Children

In conclusion, taking your 5- to 10-year-old kids on nature excursions and camping trips is not only a fun and exciting way to spend quality family time but also an invaluable opportunity to create life-changing experiences. Engaging your children in outdoor activities, exploring wilderness areas, and immersing them in the natural world can have profound and lasting effects on their physical, mental, and emotional well-being.

By finding suitable wilderness spots and carefully planning activities that cater to your children's interests and abilities, you are fostering a sense of curiosity, wonder, and appreciation for the environment. These experiences not only teach kids essential life skills such as problem-solving, communication, and teamwork but also help them develop a strong connection to nature that can last a lifetime.

Creating and sharing nutritious meals around a campfire can bring families closer together as they bond over the simple pleasures of outdoor cooking and dining. These shared experiences, coupled with the unique challenges and rewards of camping, can strengthen family bonds and create lasting memories that your children will cherish for years to come.

By teaching your children the principles of *Leave No Trace* and responsible camping, you are instilling in them a sense of stewardship and respect for the environment. This heightened awareness and under-standing of our impact on nature can inspire them to become advocates for conservation and environmental preservation in the future.

Ultimately, the experiences and lessons gained from spending time in nature can shape your children's perspectives, values, and priorities. These outdoor adventures can help them develop a sense of self-reliance, resilience, and resourcefulness that will serve them well throughout their lives. Furthermore, nurturing a love for the outdoors in your children can encourage them to seek out more opportunities to explore, learn, and grow in nature, thus fostering a lifelong passion for adventure and discovery.

As parents, it's crucial to seize the opportunity to introduce your children to the wonders of the natural world. By taking the time to research and plan, gather the necessary gear and resources, and share in the joy and excitement of outdoor experiences, you are laying the foundation for a lifetime of appreciation and respect for the environment.

So, take the leap and embark on a journey into the great outdoors with your children. The memories, lessons, and bonds formed during these adventures will not only enrich your family's life but also contribute to the development of well-rounded, environmentally conscious individuals who carry a deep love for nature and a desire to protect it for generations to come.

Notes and Plans

About the Author
Emanuel Rose: A Man of Many Passions

Emanuel Rose is a multi-talented individual, renowned as an author, outdoorsman, and marketing expert. His passion for nature has been a steady presence throughout his life, which has fueled his love for exploring forests and oceans. This lifelong fascination with the natural world inspired him to write the children's book series, *Wenaha Henry*.

In addition to his love for nature, Emanuel has embraced personal growth and meditation as essential components of his life. Through meditation, he stays grounded and centered, even during challenging times. This practice has unlocked new dimensions of creativity and intuition, which have significantly impacted his writing.

With over three decades of experience in the marketing world, Emanuel has helped numerous companies achieve success from the ground up. His innovative approach to branding, advertising, and daily operations at his digital agency, Strategic eMarketing, has solidified his status as an industry leader. Emanuel is grateful for the chance to assist others in their businesses and finds it rewarding to witness his clients attain their objectives.

Emanuel is eager to share his insights on personal growth, meditation, and the *Wenaha Henry* children's book series. If you're interested in interviewing him for your podcast, he would be honored to engage in a conversation with you. Reach out to Emanuel Rose to discuss potential collaborations. He looks forward to connecting with you soon!

Emanuel Rose's multifaceted life as an author, outdoorsman, and marketing expert has undoubtedly left a lasting impression on those who have crossed paths with him. His dedication to personal growth, meditation, and helping others succeed makes him a genuinely inspiring individual. Don't miss the opportunity to learn from his experiences and wisdom by connecting with him today at *www.emanuelrose.com*

Please support these organizations

Camp Jack Hazard

Deschutes River Alliance

Friends of the Teton River

Tom Brown, Jr.'s Tracker School

Ducks Unlimited

The Nature Conservancy

Other Children's Books by Emanuel Rose

Wenaha Henry Seeds to a Tree

Wenaha Henry Seeds to a Tree Coloring Book for Kids

Wenaha Henry Seeds to a Tree and the Grouse

Wenaha Henry Seeds to a Tree Book $44.95
Wenaha Henry Children's Coloring Book   6.99
Order: wenahahenry.com

Made in the USA
Monee, IL
23 July 2023